W9-AXI-714

4/15

$2/k$

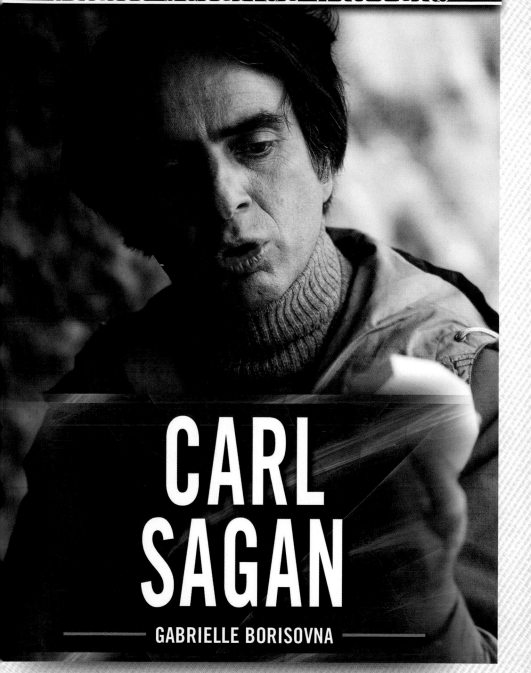

CARL SAGAN

GABRIELLE BORISOVNA

ROSEN
PUBLISHING

New York

Published in 2015 by The Rosen Publishing Group, Inc.
29 East 21st Street, New York, NY 10010

First Edition

Library of Congress Cataloging-in-Publication Data

Borisovna, Gabrielle, author.
Carl Sagan/Gabrielle Borisovna.
    pages cm.—(Great science writers)
Includes bibliographical references and index.
ISBN 978-1-4777-7681-0 (library bound)
1. Sagan, Carl, 1934-1996—Juvenile literature. 2.
Astronomers—United States—Biography—Juvenile
literature. I. Title.
QB36.S15B67 2001
520.92—dc23
[B]

                                                    2013039272

Manufactured in China

CONTENTS

INTRODUCTION

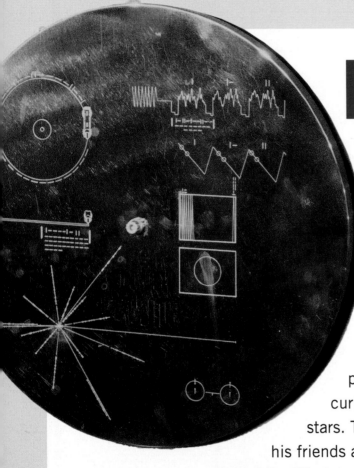

It all began with the stars.

In 1939, in Brooklyn, there lived a bright five-year-old boy named Carl Sagan. Like all children, he had questions about the world around him. In particular, he was curious about the stars. The boy asked his friends and neighbors to explain: What are the stars? How can they shine so brightly? But he found their vague answers unconvincing. So he went home and asked his mother to tell him about the stars. She told him to go to the library and find out for himself.

Carl Sagan was a scientist, a teacher, and an important figure in the story of mankind's engagement with the stars.

When Sagan asked the librarian for a book about stars, she brought him a book about Hollywood actors. The serious young boy was embarrassed and explained that those weren't the types of stars he was interested in.

Finally young Sagan got his hands on a children's book about stars. He read that the sun is a star, the center of our solar system. The other stars are massive celestial fireballs, far larger than Earth, many much larger than the sun, but so far away that, to us, they look like tiny points of light in the great dark of the sky.

The boy's imagination caught fire as he realized for the very first time the immensity of space—the sheer scale of the universe. He never forgot the breathtaking grandeur of that vision.

Fast-forward several decades, to 1990. Carl Sagan, now a famous astronomer and author, is an adviser to NASA's space program. He has been involved for years in helping to design the experiments carried out by manned and robotic space missions.

As the *Voyager* probe approaches the outer reaches of the solar system, Sagan urges his colleagues at NASA to have the probe turn its camera around and photograph Earth as it appears from approximately 3.7 billion miles away. Earth is barely visible, a tiny "pale blue dot" in a great black night.

The photograph doesn't give NASA's scientists any new data about space or about Earth. But it serves another purpose: to communicate Sagan's childhood vision of the great vastness of space. (Sagan's inspiring words about that historic photograph are discussed later.)

As one of history's great science writers, Sagan had a passion for inspiring ordinary people to marvel at the infinite frontier of space and the practical wonders of science. This is his story.

CHAPTER ONE

AN ASTRONOMER GROWS IN BROOKLYN

C arl Sagan was born in Brooklyn, New York, in 1934. His parents were both from Jewish immigrant families who fled hunger, prejudice, and persecution in eastern Europe.

SAMUEL SAGAN

Carl's father, Samuel Sagan, was born in the eastern European region known as the Pale of Settlement, often referred to as the Pale, the only area of Imperial Russia where Jews were allowed to settle permanently. During the late nineteenth and early twentieth centuries, many Jews left the Pale to escape poverty and anti-Semitism and settled in America.

The Sagan family came to America in 1910, when Samuel was five years old. When he was old enough to work, Sam went to work for his uncle George at the New York Girl Coat Company. Sam

This turn-of-the-century scene of Rowno, in Ukraine, shows Jewish refugees leaving their homes for a better life outside the Pale. The Pale region extended across what is now western Russia, as well as Poland, Ukraine, Moldova, Lithuania, and Belarus.

started out on the factory floor, but he was eventually promoted to become a manager. Sam was a gentle and good-humored man, who easily connected with others—especially his future wife, Rachel Molly Gruber.

RACHEL SAGAN

Rachel's parents came to New York City from the Austro-Hungarian Empire. A family rumor stated that

Rachel's father, Leib, had run off to America after killing an anti-Semite. When Leib had earned enough money to send for his wife, Chaiya, she joined him in the United States. In 1907, the couple had a daughter, Rachel, but Chaiya died giving birth to her next child. Unable to handle his young daughter alone, Leib sent Rachel back to his relatives in Austria. Before long, they sent young Rachel right back to New York.

Unfortunately, Leib had remarried, and his new wife couldn't stand Rachel, who had to grow up quickly. Rachel developed a sharp tongue and learned how to fight for what she wanted. She also learned how to be loyal to those who truly loved her—like Samuel Sagan.

FAMILY LIFE

After a whirlwind courtship, Rachel and Sam were married. Their firstborn, Carl, was born on November 9, 1934. Starved for love as a child, Rachel poured her whole heart into raising her son. She pushed him, cheered him on, bragged about him, and was incredibly proud of him. In fact, Rachel and Carl were so close that many other women in Carl's life found themselves intimidated by his mother. Sam and Rachel had a second child, Carol "Cari" Mae, in 1941.

Rachel was a charismatic, intelligent, ambitious, and complicated woman. She had an analytical mind and taught her children to ask tough questions about the world around them. She could be hypercritical, a perfectionist. Carl grew up a very serious, well-behaved child who followed his parents' rules without complaint.

FALLING IN LOVE WITH LEARNING

During the early decades of the twentieth century, many Jewish immigrants believed education was the key to unlocking opportunity in the new world. Carl's parents pushed him to excel in school, and he did not disappoint them. Unlike previous generations of his family, Carl would have the chance to become anything he wanted to be.

Carl's parents encouraged his interest in mathematics and science. Although they didn't have a lot of money, they bought him toy chemistry sets and electric trains. They encouraged his interest in dinosaurs, outer space, and ancient myths and legends.

Young Carl fell in love with science fiction and comics. He read books by authors like Edgar Rice Burroughs, famous for his tales of adventure set in outer space. Young Sagan's imagination was particularly sparked by tales of contact with extraterrestrials.

Edgar Rice Burroughs wrote many adventure books starring his original character Tarzan, including such titles as *Tarzan at the Earth's Core* and *Tarzan and the Leopard Men*. This is the cover of a French edition of one of Burroughs's Tarzan novels.

As an adult, Sagan would use real-life science to search for life on other planets.

When he turned thirteen, Carl prepared for his bar mitzvah, the ceremony that marks a Jewish boy's passage into manhood with him publicly reading and commenting on the Torah (Jewish bible.) However, Carl had already adopted a skeptical attitude toward the ancient Hebrew texts. He was constantly looking for ways to determine whether or not Old Testament stories had actually happened. Sagan would clash with religious fundamentalists throughout his career and would argue consistently that science, not religion, is humanity's greatest tool for learning about the universe.

MOVING ON UP

As World War II caused the garment industry to boom, Samuel Sagan climbed the career ladder at the New York Girl Coat Company. In 1948, he moved his family to the industrial factory town of Rahway, New Jersey.

It is perhaps not surprising that Carl excelled at Rahway High School, getting good grades easily. Among his many extracurricular activities were debate team, French club, journalism club, and National Honor Society. He also entered essay contests and performed in the school play—experiences that foreshadowed his later activities as an author and television personality.

NEW YORK WORLD'S FAIR

When Carl was five years old, he visited the 1939 New York City World's Fair with his parents. It was a formative experience—for years afterward, he collected souvenirs from the fair.

The World's Fair was a massive, temporary exhibition featuring many different attractions—from the Lagoon of Nations, which included pavilions hosted by various foreign countries, to exhibits presented by America's biggest corporations, to fairground attractions like Little Miracle Town, a village of little people. Held at the height of the Great Depression, when Europe was succumbing to Nazi conquest, the World's Fair communicated a simple message in exhibit after exhibit: in the future, science and technology would make the world happier, healthier, and wealthier. Young Carl, just five years old, was thrilled by the fair's portrayal of the America of the future, where cities were powered by nuclear energy and connected by a brand-new highway system, and every home would feature that cutting-edge invention, television.

One attraction would stay with Sagan for the rest of his life: the time capsule. As part of the World's Fair, a time capsule containing artifacts of life in the United States in the

1930s, along with a message for the people of earth in 6939, was buried. Sagan was awed by the idea of how much time would pass while the time capsule waited to be rediscovered. He loved the idea that to the people of the future, the everyday items in the time capsule would seem like the exotic relics of a lost civilization. As an adult, Sagan would go on to create his own time capsule: the gold record placed aboard the *Voyager* space probe.

A view of the 1939 World's Fair in Flushing Meadows, Corona, Queens. The dome in the distance is the Perisphere, which contained a massive model of an ideal future city called Democracity.

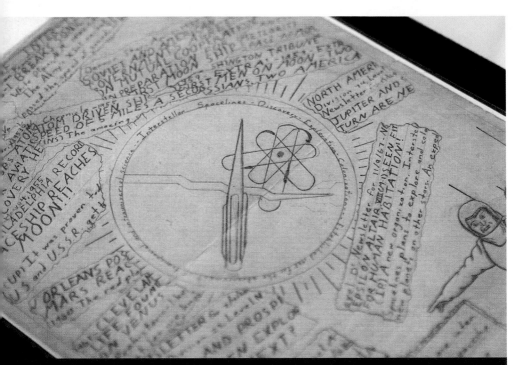

Sagan never lost his childlike wonder about the possibility of interstellar space travel. This sketch is preserved in the Carl Sagan Papers collection displayed at the Library of Congress in Washington, D.C., in 2013.

But science remained Sagan's focus. In his downtime, Sagan tinkered in his basement chemistry lab and wrote essays speculating about the existence of life on other planets. In his high school yearbook, Sagan was voted Most Likely to Succeed. According to Keay Davidson's *Carl Sagan: A Life*, the yearbook also commented poetically on his scientific ambitions:

Astronomy research is Carl's main aim,
An excellent student, he should achieve fame.

HIGHER EDUCATION

C arl Sagan was just sixteen years old when he entered the University of Chicago. There, he dove into classes designed to give students a firm grounding in the Western tradition, from classics to literature to philosophy to history, as well as science and math. Sagan discovered a talent for grasping the big ideas that had shaped Western civilization.

Sagan was determined to learn all the subjects that could help him locate life on other planets—not just astronomy, but physics, chemistry, and biology, too. He progressed quickly, taking full advantage of all the different levels of study his university had to offer. Sagan received his A.B. with honors in 1954, and his bachelor of science in physics in 1955. In 1956, he earned his master of science in physics. That same year, he entered the university's astronomy Ph.D. program. Just four years later, he earned his Ph.D. in astronomy and astrophysics.

Carl Sagan was able to study astronomy seriously for the first time at the University of Chicago. While he focused on science, his studies in the humanities helped make him a great science writer.

Sagan was fortunate enough to work with several very impressive mentors. Here are a few of the scientists whose ideas and friendship shaped Sagan.

H. J. MULLER (1890–1967)

In the summer of 1952, Sagan worked with Nobel Prize–winning geneticist H. J. Muller at Indiana University. Muller is most famous for proving that X-rays can damage or mutate genes, revealing just how dangerous it is to expose life-forms to radiation, particularly radiation given off by nuclear weapons. Later in life, Sagan himself would become a fierce opponent of nuclear weapons.

Sagan worked in Muller's lab checking fruit flies for mutations. He didn't love the work, but he greatly admired Muller; the two men bonded over their love of wild ideas and their shared interest in the origins of life.

H. C. UREY (1893–1981)

Sagan's interest in the origins of life also led him to study with University of Chicago professor H. C. Urey. Urey was a Nobel Prize–wining chemist, one of the pioneers of cosmochemistry, the study of what chemicals exist in the universe and how they developed. Urey's work was in service of finding the origins of

Harold Urey in his laboratory. His discovery of deuterium earned him the 1934 Nobel Prize for Chemistry. He had a complicated relationship with the young Sagan, whose arrogance irked him.

the solar system and of Earth. He had a special interest in the origins of life on Earth.

As an undergraduate, Sagan took the first chance he got to study with Urey, and he was foolhardy enough to write a paper on the origins of life. Urey criticized the paper harshly, forcing Sagan to rewrite it completely. Sagan continued to work on the paper for years.

Urey found Sagan bright but undisciplined. The two had a complicated relationship; Urey felt that Sagan sometimes disrespected him or disregarded his advice. However, later in life, Urey came to respect Sagan as a science popularizer.

GERARD KUIPER (1905–1973)

Astronomer Gerard Kuiper was the head of the University of Chicago's astronomy Ph.D. program. Kuiper has many claims to fame, such as discovering moons of the planets Uranus and Neptune, and discovering that Titan, one of Saturn's moons, had an atmosphere. Sagan worked with Kuiper at McDonald Observatory in Fort Davis, Texas, in the summer of 1956. Later, Sagan pursued his Ph.D. under Kuiper at the Yerkes Observatory in Williams Bay, Wisconsin.

Sagan did not love working in observatories. Places like Fort Davis and Williams Bay were sleepy and remote—good for dark skies but not for stimulating company. Sagan found taking astronomical observations tedious. He would become a theoretician, a scientist more focused on formulating ideas than collecting data.

Gerard Kuiper at the Yerkes Observatory. Sagan's first really in-depth work in an observatory occurred under Kuiper's supervision.

GEORGE GAMOW (1904–1968)

In the summer of 1957, Sagan traveled to the University of Colorado at Boulder to work with famous scientist George Gamow. Gamow was primarily a theoretical physicist, but he studied many different questions, from how stars are formed to how the universe began. He was also interested in molecular genetics.

MELVIN CALVIN (1911–1997)

Melvin Calvin won the Nobel Prize in Chemistry for discovering the Calvin cycle in 1961, which described the process by which plants use photosynthesis to absorb carbon. Sagan spent the summer of 1959 working at Calvin's lab in Berkeley, California. Like Sagan's other mentors, Calvin was interested in the origins of life and wondered whether or not extraterrestrial life was possible.

GRADUATE SCHOOL YEARS

As a graduate student, Sagan started to develop his personality as a showman. He offered occasional Saturday lectures at the Yerkes observatory, and he organized a lecture series on the main University of Chicago campus called "The Creation of Life in the

THE ORIGINS OF LIFE

Sagan's deep interest in extraterrestrial life led him to wonder just exactly how life on Earth had originated. Over and over again during his studies, he worked with scientists who were asking questions such as: Just how did life evolve on Earth? Did the organic building blocks of life form spontaneously on Earth, or were they cosmic hijackers that arrived on our planet via a comet or meteorite? What were the conditions that allowed life to arise on our planet? If these questions were answered, scientists could search for other places in the universe likely to be suitable for the development of life.

Among the experiments that inspired Sagan was the Miller-Urey experiment, which was conducted at the University of Chicago while Sagan was an undergraduate. Urey and Stanley Miller created an enclosed mini-environment that simulated the atmosphere and chemical composition of the early Earth, then used electricity to spark chemical reactions that would create organic building blocks of life. The experiment succeeded in forming organic compounds, including amino acids and sugars, giving Sagan hope that it might be just a few short years before scientists could determine how life originated on Earth. Sadly, he was too optimistic; the origins of life on Earth remain a subject for research, speculation, and study to this day.

Universe," featuring talks by the many distinguished scientists whom Sagan had befriended. The lecture series demonstrated Sagan's passion for introducing the public to important new ideas. It also convinced many of his teachers and fellow students that Sagan was a little arrogant.

Ambitious Sagan tried to synthesize all of his graduate experiences and studies in his 1960 Ph.D. thesis, "Physical Studies of the Planets." The thesis touches on the possibility that organic molecules might exist on the moon, the search for organic molecules on Jupiter, and radiation coming from the surface of Venus.

SOCIAL LIFE: LYNN

Sagan worked hard at the University of Chicago, but he did have a social life. In fact, it was there that he met his first wife, Lynn Alexander. Later she went by Lynn Margulis, and she was a famous biologist.

Carl met Lynn when he was twenty and she was just sixteen. She wasn't new on campus, however—she had gained admittance to the university at the tender age of fourteen. Carl and Lynn struck up a conversation in the math building. Lynn was just as intelligent as Carl, with a lively interest in all sorts of subjects. The couple married on June 16, 1957.

While Carl was pursuing his Ph.D., Lynn was forging her own career as a scientist. This was somewhat unusual in the 1950s, when not many women pursued careers in science. Indeed, many people expected women to give up their careers altogether in order to get married and start a family. The couple had two children: Dorion Solomon Sagan, born in 1959, and Jeremy Ethan Sagan, born in 1960.

Unfortunately, Lynn and Carl's relationship suffered after their children arrived. Like many men of his era, Sagan expected his wife to take care of him and had no interest in splitting household chores or childrearing responsibilities. Lynn found herself struggling to balance her scientific career with the running of the entire Sagan household. Eventually, they both found that they just couldn't make the marriage work. Lynn left Carl in 1962.

Today, Lynn is best known for her work on endosymbiosis. She advanced the idea that early life

SPUTNIK

In the wake of World War II, the global map was redrawn, leaving two superpowers—the United States and the Soviet Union (U.S.S.R.)—with competing political philosophies and interests wrestling for influence over the globe. The superpowers never went to war directly with each other; instead they engaged in a "Cold War." This involved proxy conflicts in third world countries, where rival factions backed by different powers battled, and an arms race. It even extended into space.

At first, the U.S.S.R. was the front-runner in the so-called space race. Soviets achieved many important firsts—but the most significant was the one that started it all. In October 1957, while Sagan was a Ph.D. astronomy student, the Soviet Union successfully launched the very first satellite to achieve a controlled orbit of Earth, *Sputnik*. Ordinary Americans watched *Sputnik's* blinking light travel across the night sky and worried that their country was falling behind. Concern over *Sputnik* helped to jumpstart America's space program, NASA, creating the opportunity for scientists like Carl Sagan to explore outer space.

Biologist Lynn Margulis is seen in a greenhouse in this 1990 photograph. Sagan's first wife, Margulis is perhaps even more respected than Sagan in scientific circles.

forms "joined forces" in order to survive. The most famous example is the mitochondria, the "batteries" that power many cells by creating ATP, which produces cellular energy. These mitochondria have their own DNA and were once independent bacteria. Absorbed into larger cells, they provide power while benefiting from a sheltered environment. Lynn argued that cooperation might be as important as competition in explaining the history of life on Earth.

CHAPTER THREE

STARTING LIFE IN THE REAL WORLD

I n 1960, armed with a brand-new Ph.D., Carl Sagan set out to begin his life as a scientist. He was fortunate enough to win the Miller Fellowship, a prestigious two-year-long postdoctoral fellowship at the University of California at Berkeley.

BERKELEY

It was an interesting time and place. In some ways, the San Francisco Bay Area was already beginning to develop the nonconformist, rebellious culture that would come into full flower in the 1967 "Summer of Love." Sagan, who had found himself frustrated by the tight-laced culture at observatories like Yerkes and McDonald, enjoyed this relaxed atmosphere. Later in his career, he would become known as a "hip" scientist—someone who could speak to young people and ordinary folks, not just fellow eggheads with advanced degrees.

In California, Sagan worked on a wide variety of projects. He wrote scientific papers, worked with NASA, and became an associate editor of a new astronomy magazine called *Icarus*. He also worked with Nobel Prize–winning geneticist Joshua Lederberg at Stanford University.

Best of all, Sagan's fellowship helped him to land a job at the most prestigious university in the country.

HARVARD

Sagan's first true job as an academic was at Harvard, where he was an assistant professor of astronomy from 1962 until 1968. He developed a reputation as an engaging and enjoyable professor. However, Sagan wasn't comfortable interacting with other faculty members. He felt more at ease in the classroom— where he was the most important person in the room.

However, Sagan did launch two important scientific collaborations at Harvard. One was with chemist Bishun Khare, who answered a classified ad Sagan had placed in *Physics Today* seeking someone to work on interdisciplinary projects involving physics, physical and organic chemistry, and more. If Sagan was a theoretician who liked to sketch out ideas on paper, Khare was a passionate lab scientist who helped Sagan to test his theories. Their partnership would last for decades.

VENUS

During Sagan's time in California, he did important work on the atmosphere of Venus. In a 1961 article for *Science* magazine, Sagan gave an overview of past scientists' ideas about what the surface of Venus might be like. Because of the planet's cloud cover, mere telescope observation could not reveal much about Venus. Was it a planet covered in oceans, jungles, or deserts? Sagan believed that Venus was subject to a greenhouse effect, which made the planet's surface extremely hot. However, he imagined that the upper atmosphere might be cool enough to host microorganisms. If the clouds of Venus contained water, perhaps humans could one day "terraform" Venus, putting microorganisms from Earth into the upper atmosphere to create oxygen, decreasing the carbon dioxide in the atmosphere, and eventually cooling down the planet's atmosphere. The article was classic Sagan: a mix of wonderful prose, bold ideas, hard science, and some wild speculation.

This photograph *(right)* was taken by the *Pioneer* Venus Orbiter in 1979. The cloud formations above Venus once gave astronomers hope that Venus was a watery planet; since then scientists have discovered that the clouds are made of sulphuric acid.

The other important collaboration Sagan launched at Harvard was with graduate student Jim Pollack. The two worked together on developing Sagan's ideas about Mars and would continue collaborating throughout their careers. Pollack went on to become an extremely respected astronomer in his own right.

MARS

For centuries, mankind had observed the surface of Mars. Some early astronomers gazing through their telescopes saw what looked to them like polar ice caps, or oceans on the surface of the red planet. Others saw ridgelike lines that they assumed were canals, perhaps evidence of an advanced civilization.

Astronomers had often noted that the surface of Mars seemed to get darker from time to time. Earlier scientists had wondered if the darkening was caused by vegetation undergoing seasonal changes. Sagan proposed a different solution: he believed that the darkening was caused by dust storms, blowing dust from one area to another. This important prediction was later confirmed by probes of the red planet.

But Sagan did not rule out the idea that life might exist on Mars. In the early 1960s, Pollack and Sagan created "Mars jars," tiny self-contained microenvironments designed to mimic the Martian atmosphere. Their goal was to see if organic molecules, the building blocks of life, could arise independently on Mars. Sagan also introduced microorganisms into his Mars jars, to see if Terran (Earth-like) life forms could survive in the Martian environment. Some microorganisms did survive, encouraging Sagan.

A NEW LOVE

While at Harvard, Sagan met his second wife, Linda Salzman. Linda and Carl epitomized the old saying "opposites attract." While Carl was an analytical, logical scientist, Linda was a free-spirited, fun-loving, intuitive artist. They were married in 1968. Sagan's friend Lester Grinspoon, a Harvard psychiatry professor, served as his best man, and one of the official witnesses was Sagan's friend Isaac Asimov, the great science fiction writer.

In 1970, Linda and Carl welcomed their son Nicholas Julian Zapata Sagan. His middle names came from civil rights activist and African American lawmaker Julian Bond, and from Emiliano Zapata, one of the leaders of the Mexican Revolution and a fighter for peasant rights.

Carl and Linda collaborated a bit together; they worked together on creating the plaque that NASA

SAGAN AND THE SIXTIES

The era that most people mean when they refer to "the sixties"—civil rights, counterculture, hippies, free love, Vietnam protests, rock 'n'roll—did not really begin until the middle of that decade. Sagan was teaching at Harvard during that time. While he was somewhat isolated within his ivory tower, Sagan was touched by the spirit of the times.

In 1963, during the civil rights era, Sagan traveled to Alabama, where he participated in civil rights marches and protested against racial segregation. And in 1965, Sagan made a point of traveling to guest lecture on astronomy at Alabama's all-black Tuskegee Institute.

Sagan's stance against the Vietnam War led him, in 1966, to resign from the U.S. Air Force Scientific Advisory Board's Geophysics Panel. He took this step despite the fact that he did not work on Vietnam-related issues; he simply wanted nothing more to do with the military. This was a big deal for Sagan, as he received a great deal of money from military sources such as the RAND Corporation, a military think tank.

Vietnam, of course, was part of the greater global Cold War between the United States and the U.S.S.R. Sagan made a strong statement for international peace by publishing a book, *Intelligent Life in the Universe*, coauthored in 1966 with Soviet Russian author I. S. Shklovskii. This collaboration between scientists from rival countries highlighted the similarities, not the differences, between the superpowers.

placed on the *Pioneer 10* probe, as well as on producing the golden *Voyager* record. However, over time the differences between Carl and Linda started to wear at their relationship. Once again, Carl's disinterest in prioritizing his home and family life placed a strain on the couple. Sagan left Linda for another woman in 1977, although their bitter divorce was not finalized until 1981.

NO TENURE FOR YOU

In most universities, professors who have proved that they contribute significantly to their fields are granted tenure. A tenured professor is a permanent member of the faculty and will not be fired without just cause. In 1967, Carl Sagan came up for tenure at Harvard. Although it is notoriously hard to get tenure

With his trademark turtleneck; his interest in far-out theories, UFOs, and space travel; and his references to mythology, Sagan was considered a "hip" astronomer by members of the counterculture in the 1960s and 1970s.

the review. As a backup, Sagan was being seriously considered for a job at MIT.

However, not everybody loved Sagan. Some colleagues saw him as arrogant, egotistical, and pretentious. Others were a bit uncomfortable with how much attention Sagan got from the press—Sagan was often contacted by journalists for quotes about astronomy, the space race, and the possibility of life elsewhere in the universe. Then there was the question of Sagan's recommendations. Asked by MIT and Harvard to comment on Sagan's work, his mentor Urey complained that Sagan's interests were too far-ranging and that his approach to research was not rigorous enough.

Sagan was denied tenure at Harvard, and he was not offered a job at MIT. Instead, he took a post at another Ivy League university, Cornell, located in Ithaca, New York.

CORNELL

Sagan began teaching at Cornell in 1968. He also served as director of Cornell's Laboratory for Planetary Studies, as well as associate director of the Center for Radio Physics and Space Research. In addition, Sagan taught a course on critical thinking, which he offered until his death. He received tenure at Cornell in 1971.

It was at Cornell that Sagan started to truly commit to his work as a popularizer of science, writing

Sagan in a Cornell University lab in 1974. Sagan had a hard time fitting in at Harvard, but the faculty at Cornell honored and respected him.

books, appearing on television, and working with Hollywood directors. He also exposed crackpot pseudoscientists and engaged in political activism.

In the upcoming sections, we will take a closer look at a few of the fields Sagan made his mark on.

CHAPTER FOUR

SAGAN AND SPACE EXPLORATION

C arl Sagan began working with NASA as an adviser in 1959. He would work for and champion the space agency until his death. He was also involved in other programs and activities that explored space, such as SETI, the search for extraterrestrial intelligence.

Here's a closer look at some of the major ways Sagan influenced mankind's ventures into space.

MARINER 2 (1962)

Sagan was deeply involved in NASA's 1962 *Mariner 2* mission to study the atmosphere of Venus. He helped develop scientific instruments that would allow scientists to get a closer look at Venus's upper reaches. While the probe confirmed Sagan's theories that Venus was heated by a greenhouse effect, it also discovered that Venus was hellishly hot—crushing Sagan's hope that life might be discovered there.

APOLLO 11 MOON
LANDING (1969)

Sagan helped to plan America's greatest space race triumph, the moment in 1969 when astronauts actually walked on the surface of the moon. Sagan was among those who briefed the Apollo astronauts, Neil Armstrong, Buzz Aldrin, and Michael Collins, before they left for their historic mission.

Of course now every child knows that the moon is a lifeless rock. But before the moon landing, there

The 1969 *Apollo 11* moon landing. Here, astronaut Buzz Aldrin conducts a scientific experiment. Aldrin was one of the speakers at Sagan's memorial service.

was still some hope that when the astronauts landed, they might find lunar organic materials or perhaps even microscopic life-forms. Sagan and his colleagues feared that if indigenous life did exist on the moon, the astronauts might bring microorganisms with them from Earth that could endanger lunar life-forms. They were also worried that the astronauts could unwittingly bring some dangerous lunar life-form back with them from space. Because of these concerns, NASA decided to take the expensive precaution of sterilizing all of the equipment that would touch the moon's surface. Astronauts Armstrong and Aldrin also spent several weeks in quarantine on Earth before they were allowed to reemerge.

It turned out that these precautions were unnecessary. When Sagan and other scientists examined the rocks that the astronauts collected, they found absolutely no signs of life. Sagan was unapologetic: better safe than sorry.

PIONEER 10 AND *11* (1969–1970)

Sagan helped NASA to plan the missions of *Pioneer 10* and *Pioneer 11*, the first spacecraft that left our solar system. Journalist Eric Burgess suggested that since *Pioneer 10* would be the first manmade object to reach the outer limits of the solar system, perhaps NASA should attach a plaque to it, as a message to any extraterrestrials it might encounter. Needless to say, Sagan loved the idea.

Sagan worked on the plaque's design with his friend and colleague, fellow astrophysicist Frank Drake. They decided that *Pioneer 11* should give directions back to earth. But how? What point of reference might we possibly share with distant alien beings? Drake and Sagan drew a map of the location of the sun in relation to the nearest pulsars, or neutron stars that rotate, emitting radiation as they turn. The plaque also included the pulsars' rates of rotation, trusting that an alien intelligent enough to decode their message could locate the pulsars in question. Another diagram showed the solar system and the path of *Pioneer* as it traveled into space.

It was Linda Salzman's idea to add pictures to the plaque: a man with his hand extended in greeting and behind him, a woman. She herself drew the pictures of humanity that would be our first emissaries to the stars.

The plaque captured the public's imagination— and raised hackles across the political spectrum. Because the human figures on the plaque were naked, some considered the plaque shameful. Others decided that the plaque was subtly sexist (since the man was greeting ETs while the woman hung back) or Eurocentric (since both figures appeared to be white).

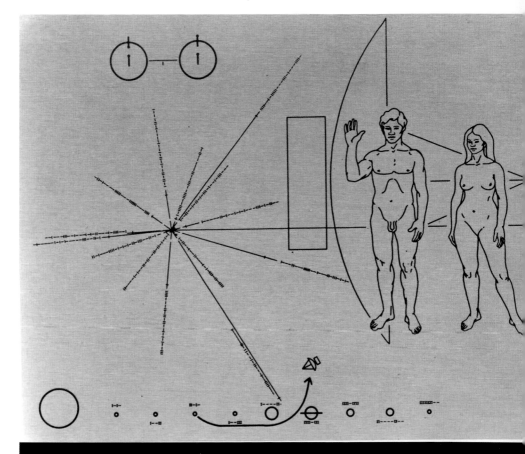

The image affixed to the *Pioneer 10* spacecraft, designed by Carl Sagan, Linda Sagan, and Frank Drake. Launched in March 1972, *Pioneer 10* has now traveled billions of miles into space.

Sagan and his team had tried to make their message universal; the idea that it might privilege one human group over another pained them. Sagan swore that if he ever sent another message to the stars, he would be more careful.

MARINER 9 (1971) AND VIKING (1975)

1971's *Mariner 9* was designed to orbit above the surface of Mars, mapping the terrain below. *Mariner 9* confirmed that Sagan's theory about Martian dust storms causing waves of darkening was correct; in fact, when *Mariner 9* began its orbit, the probe could not see through a thick dust storm. When the dust cleared, another one of Sagan's ideas was confirmed. Along with Jim Pollack, Sagan had predicted that the surface of Mars was not smooth (as some scientists believed) but contained peaks and valleys. *Mariner 9*

A test version of the *Viking* Mars Lander, displayed at NASA's Jet Propulsion Laboratory. The Lander took photographs, collected data, and carried out scientific experiments.

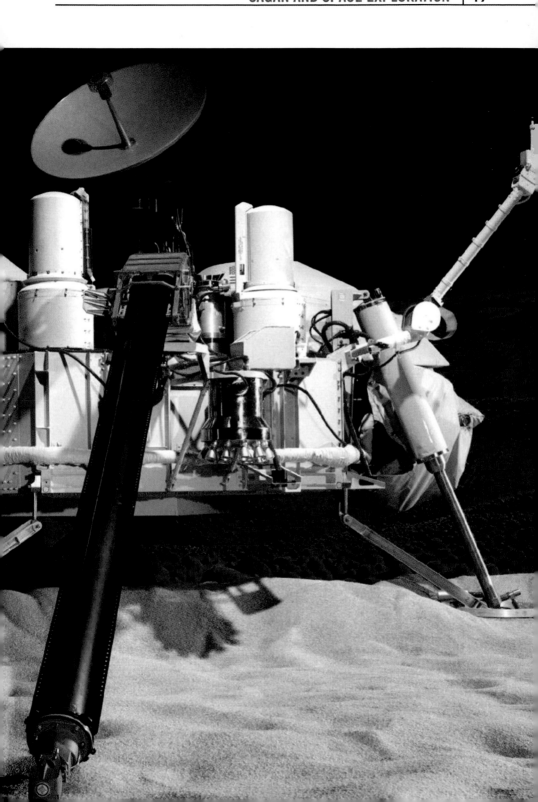

discovered that Mars had mountains higher than Mount Everest and gorges many times deeper than the Grand Canyon. Moreover, the landscape was crossed by what appeared to be dried-up riverbeds.

In 1975, the *Viking* mission landed two stationary spacecraft on the surface of Mars. Sagan participated in NASA scientists' discussions about where the spacecraft should land and what kind of scientific equipment they should bring with them. He was so excited about the possibility that *Viking* might find life on Mars that he made sure the craft carried cameras capable of photographing moving objects. Unfortunately for Sagan, the *Viking* craft spotted no life-forms; indeed, the soils the *Vikings* collected contained no biosignatures, or signs of life.

VOYAGER (1977)

The *Voyager* probe was supposed to travel past Jupiter, past Saturn, leaving the solar system and venturing into the vast frontier of space. Sagan sensed a chance to send another message to the stars—and this time, he wanted to do more than simply give ETs a map back to Earth. He wanted to make a statement about life on our planet that would be meaningful to hypothetical extraterrestrials and real earthlings alike.

To create the record, Sagan assembled a team of friends and colleagues including Frank Drake, Linda Sagan, artist Jon Lomberg, and folklorist/ethnomusicologist Alan Lomax. There were also two other very important members of the team: Sagan's friend, writer Timothy Ferris, and Ferris's fiancée, the beautiful and intelligent Ann Druyan, who would become the love of Sagan's life.

Together, the team created the *Voyager* Interstellar Record. Designed to last for millions of years, the

The golden record affixed to the *Voyager* probe in 1977. While the disc was engraved with a graphic, it was the record's encoded audio and image information that contained the real message to the stars.

golden record encoded sights and sounds from Earth. Music included ranged from Bach to Senegalese drumming, from Louis Armstrong to Indian raga. Other sounds included whale songs, volcanoes erupting, laughter, and a rocket launch. There were also simple greetings in a myriad of human languages. The Persian greeting translates as: "Hello, to the residents of far skies." In the Amoy language, from Southern Fujian, the greeting went, "Friends of space, how are you all? Have you eaten yet? Come visit us if you have time." The English greeting was Sagan's own young son Nick saying "Hello from the children of planet Earth."

The record also included images of the solar system, anatomical diagrams of humans, plus images of a seashell, a gymnast, the Great Wall of China, an astronaut in space, and more. The making of the record was documented in the book *Murmurs of Earth* (1978.)

ARE WE ALONE IN THE UNIVERSE?

Throughout his life, Sagan was fascinated by the possibility that intelligent life might exist elsewhere in the universe. As a teenager, he was transfixed by reports of UFOs, or unidentified flying objects. As

Sagan learned more about the scientific method and read books skeptical of UFO sightings, he realized that the UFO phenomenon was probably psychological. That is to say, most people saw UFOs because, at a time when faith in religion was at an all-time low and anxiety about the Cold War was at a perilous high, people needed something to believe in.

Sagan never ruled out the idea that extraterrestrials might visit Earth one day—he just wanted to make absolutely sure that when they did, their presence was scientifically verified, so that the world could respond properly.

Sagan became a member of the O'Brien Commission, the panel charged with advising the air force about the UFO phenomenon. He testified about UFOs in front of Congress and served as an expert witness in the criminal trial of a man who used a UFO hoax to defraud a gullible old woman. He even arranged a public debate pitting UFO believers against serious scientists.

Sagan would also write several books about the possibility of extraterrestrial life. In addition to his breakthrough 1966 book *Intelligent Life in the Universe*, cowritten with Soviet scientist Shklovskii, he also published *UFOs: a Scientific Debate* (1972, with Thorton Page) and *Communication with Extraterrestrial Intelligence* (1973).

SAGAN AND SETI

Sagan was a champion of SETI, or the search for extraterrestrial intelligence, a scientific effort to locate signs of intelligent life in the universe. In 1961, Sagan attended the very first SETI conference at the National Radio Astronomy Observatory in Green Bank, West Virginia, where host Dr. Frank Drake had already begun scanning the skies for extraterrestrial signals. Many well-respected scientists attended that first event; it had not yet become embarrassing for serious scientists to speculate about the possibility of life elsewhere in the universe. Most agreed that they should search the stars in hopes of picking up extraterrestrial signals. But where should they look? How many other intelligences were likely to be out there in the universe?

Sagan was one of the more optimistic conference attendees. He believed that there were many planets out there in the universe where the conditions for life existed—in fact, there were probably exotic life-forms out there able to exist in conditions that would kill any Terran organism. Sagan also believed that where there is life, intelligence will ultimately arise. He was convinced that if there were intelligent extraterrestrials somewhere out there, they were likely to be advanced, having moved beyond hunger, war, and other petty human problems.

Sagan would remain involved with SETI for the rest of his career. But by the 1980s, many observers—and members of Congress—were ready to give up on the SETI search. Skeptical scientists asked: if aliens exist, how come they have not already contacted us? In 1980, Sagan cofounded the Planetary Society, an organization that advocated for public funding of space research, including SETI, with Bruce Murray and Louis Friedman of NASA's Jet Propulsion Laboratory. When the SETI search was finally eliminated from the United States' national budget, Sagan helped to find private funding to continue the project. Today the SETI search continues in the private sector.

LINDA VS. CARL

As we have seen, the 1970s were a busy time for Sagan. He was teaching at Cornell, working with NASA, and, as we'll see later, writing award-winning books. Carl and Linda found that their different approaches to life were making them grow farther and farther apart.

And then, something happened. Sagan met and fell deeply in love with the woman who would become his lifelong partner, Ann Druyan.

THE ARECIBO MESSAGE

In 1974, Sagan helped to write the so-called Arecibo message, a powerful radio signal beamed out into space, intended to contact other intelligent beings. Sagan helped Frank Drake create the message.

The Arecibo message was partially ceremonial; it was broadcast into space in order to help celebrate the 1974

This 2012 photo shows the powerful radio telescope at Puerto Rico's Arecibo Observatory. Sagan and Drake returned to Arecibo in the summer of 1975 to listen for any reply to their Arecibo message. They were disappointed. We have still not heard a reply.

remodeling of the Puerto Rico's Arecibo radio telescope. The Arecibo message was aimed at a nearby star cluster called M13. The binary code message included the numbers one through ten, followed by a scientific description of DNA and a crude picture of a human, the solar system, and the radio dish itself. The radio message will take twenty-five thousand years to reach its destination.

A NEW LIFE PARTNER

Sagan and Druyan met when he was forty-two and she was nearly twenty-eight. She was an intelligent, lively writer who had spent her university years less focused on schoolwork than on activism. Everyone noticed her warmth—she had an emotional intelligence just as powerful as her sharp mind.

Sagan met Druyan through a mutual acquaintance: great screenwriter and director Nora Ephron, who was famous for making classic romantic comedies. Ephron had an idea that Sagan and Druyan might enjoy each others' company, and she invited them both to a dinner party. Sagan attended with his wife, Linda, and Druyan brought along her fiancé, writer Timothy Ferris. (Ferris and Sagan were already friends; as a journalist, Ferris had written a profile of Sagan for *Rolling Stone* magazine.) The two couples went on to become fast friends.

Sagan, Ferris, Linda, and Druyan ended up collaborating on the making of the *Voyager* interstellar record. Ann became the project's creative director. It was during this process that Sagan and Druyan fell in love.

Druyan later told Jad Abumrad and Robert Krulwich of the public radio program *Radiolab* about calling Sagan to tell him that she had found the perfect piece of Chinese music to include on their record. Sagan wasn't in his hotel room, so she left a message for him. When he called her back, he said:

I get back to my hotel room and I find this message and it says "Annie called." And I say to myself, "why didn't you leave me this message 10 years ago?"

And my heart completely skipped a beat... And I said "For keeps?" and he said, "You mean get married?" And I said, "Yes." And we had never kissed...or even had any kind of personal discussion before. We both hung up the phone, and I just screamed out loud. I remember it so well because it was this great Eureka moment. And then the phone rang... and it was Carl, and he said, "I just wanted to make sure that really happened. We're getting married, right?" And

Sagan with his third wife and soul mate, Ann Druyan. The pair had two children together and collaborated on several books and other projects.

I said, "Yeah, we're getting married." And he said, "OK, I just wanted to make sure!"

Sagan and Druyan confessed their love for each other on June 1, 1977. The date became a private code for their love for each other.

They waited until the September 5 *Voyager* launch to break the news to Timothy Ferris and to Linda Sagan. Linda was particularly shattered—not only did she feel betrayed by Carl but also by her friend Annie. Carl and Linda's divorce was bitter, fraught with legal battles over what would happen with money, custody over Nick, and many other issues.

However, most people in Carl's life agreed that Druyan changed Sagan for the better. Druyan inspired Sagan to reconcile with his older children, to reconnect with his sister, Cari, and to apologize to his first wife, Lynn, for his treatment of her during their marriage.

Sagan's divorce from Linda was finalized in May 1981. Druyan and Sagan were married soon after, on June 1. They would stay together until Sagan's death, having two children: Alexandra "Sasha" Druyan, born in 1982, and Samuel Democritus Sagan, born in 1991.

CHAPTER FIVE

SAGAN THE AUTHOR, CELEBRITY, AND TELEVISION PERSONALITY

oday, Sagan is best remembered as a science writer, broadcaster, and celebrity. In this section, we will take a look at a few of Sagan's major books, as well as his television appearances and his novel and movie *Contact*.

INTELLIGENT LIFE IN THE UNIVERSE (1966)

In 1966, Sagan published his first big break-through book, *Intelligent Life in the Universe*, cowritten with Russian I. S. Shklovskii. Sagan actually met Shklovskii through his work for the RAND Corporation. As a military think tank, RAND collected scientific and technological papers from Russia. A RAND employee noticed that Shklovskii and Sagan shared an interest in a possible greenhouse effect on Venus—actually, Shklovskii was inspired by Sagan's work on Venus. The two men began corresponding, and Shklovskii sent Sagan the manuscript of his popular astronomy book *Universe, Life, Mind*. Sagan loved the book and suggested that he might publish it in the United States along with his own contributions and thoughts. The result was a cowritten, collaborative book, *Intelligent Life in the Universe*.

At the height of the Cold War and the space race, this was a great statement: an American astronomer and a Russian scientist putting Earthly conflicts in perspective by looking to the stars. Although published by a small publishing house, the book sold well and got great reviews. Sagan became a go-to scientist for journalists looking for quotes about ETs, space discoveries, and other hot space topics.

THE COSMIC CONNECTION (1973)

Sagan's talent for communicating complicated ideas in inspiring ways caught the attention of publisher Jerome Agel, who specialized in asking interesting public figures to create slim, easy-to-read books for general audiences. Agel wanted to publish a book about outer space, and he decided that Sagan might be the right astronomer to write it. The result was Sagan's first hit book, *The Cosmic Connection: An Extraterrestrial Perspective*. The book was written

Carl Sagan on the arts television program *Camera Three* in 1974. Sagan became a popular television personality, beloved by the press for his ability to explain astronomy in simple but inspiring language.

in a personal, conversational tone—in fact, Sagan dictated much of the book into a handheld recorder while driving across the United States.

Published in 1973, *The Cosmic Connection* struck a chord with young people interested and involved in the counterculture. Science was not the most popular topic among many disaffected young people; they associated science with the military, nuclear weapons, and chemical weapons like Agent Orange. Still, there were some technologically inclined hippies who believed that technology could be used to liberate mankind and support the cause of progress. It was this segment of the counterculture that helped to give birth to the personal computer and the Internet.

The Cosmic Connection was a huge hit. *Science* reviewer William Hartmann raved that the book "ought to be read by high school and college kids, college dropouts, your nephews and nieces, anyone who ever uttered a word against science and technology, and by Richard Nixon and Gerald Ford." Other reviewers agreed. In order to promote the book, Sagan went on several television shows—including *The Tonight Show* with Johnny Carson.

LATE NIGHT IN OUTER SPACE: FRIENDSHIP WITH JOHNNY CARSON

For thirty years, Johnny Carson reigned as the king of late night television. His show hosted the biggest names in American entertainment. In the days before cable news, an appearance on *The Tonight Show* could launch a person from complete obscurity to nationwide fame overnight.

Carson was also an amateur astronomer. Once Sagan hit *The Tonight Show* stage, it quickly became clear that the charismatic astronomer would make a great repeat guest. Eloquent and good-humored,

Johnny Carson, the King of Late Night, at his front office in 1983. Although Carson hosted a variety show, he enjoyed welcoming intellectuals, scientists, and other serious public figures as guests.

with a prophetic streak, Sagan was able to laugh at Johnny's jokes, but he could also take audiences on an emotional journey. For the next two decades, he would return to *The Tonight Show* about twice a year.

The Tonight Show made Sagan a household name, and it and gave him the opportunity to reach a huge audience. Sagan was able to use his new celebrity to champion NASA funding in Congress, as well as to make important statements on significant political issues.

SAGAN AND SATIRE

As Sagan became more famous, he began to attract a little good-natured ribbing. He was parodied on *Saturday Night Live*, and he inspired Walker Percy to write a wild comic rollercoaster of a book, *Lost in the Cosmos: The Last Self Help Book*. But perhaps the most famous satire of Sagan was performed in a *Tonight Show* sketch by Sagan's friend Johnny Carson.

Carson played Sagan, making fun of Sagan's trademark soaring language and overenunciation. When asked by his straight man whether his books earned a lot of money, "Sagan" replied, "I've made billions and billions." "Billions and billions" soon caught on and became the catchphrase most associated with Carl Sagan—despite the fact that Sagan never actually uttered the words himself. Today, there is a well-known joke unit of measurement called a Sagan. A Sagan is four billion—the smallest number that could fit the description "billions and billions."

THE DRAGONS OF EDEN: SPECULATIONS ON THE EVOLUTION OF HUMAN INTELLIGENCE (1977)

Sagan's star continued to rise with *The Dragons of Eden*, his kaleidoscopic inquiry into the question of how human intelligence developed throughout history.

In the book, the relentless logician Sagan asked why the human brain is prone to such illogical expressions as dreams, irrational fears, and myths. Sagan introduces different theories about how the brain creates the mind and speculates on how our ancient myths and legends might be rooted in human evolution. The book's title, *Dragons of Eden*, refers to Sagan's idea that our legends about dragons might trace back to an ancient evolutionary fear of snakes and lizards.

The book was a huge success; almost everyone loved Sagan's lucid, entertaining prose style. There were only a few dissenting voices. In his *New York Times Book Review* article "The Brain Knew More than the Genes," Richard Restak complained that Sagan didn't back up enough of his speculations with facts, but wrote, "All in all, though, it is a thought-provoking, maddening, generally worthwhile performance that is unlikely ever to be precisely duplicated." Despite this lukewarm review (and some unenthusiastic notices in science journals like *Human Ecology*) *The Dragons of Eden* went on to win the Pulitzer Prize.

COSMOS: THE TV SERIES

Sagan's most famous, innovative, and influential production was his television series, *Cosmos*. Sagan and Druyan joined forces with astrophysicist Steven Soter to create this acclaimed thirteen-part television series, which attempted to tell the story of the universe and to locate man's place within it.

The idea for the series came from Sagan's friend, writer and engineer Gentry Lee. Worried that the public was losing interest in space, Lee decided that he and Sagan should make TV

Sagan on the set of his groundbreaking series *Cosmos*. The show went a long way toward making science accessible and attracted millions of viewers around the world.

shows and movies about science. After a little initial hesitation, Sagan agreed it was a good idea; he believed the viewing public was far more intelligent than was generally acknowledged. They called their new partnership Carl Sagan Productions.

An opportunity came when a Los Angeles public television station asked Sagan to host a miniseries called *The Heavens*. The series would follow the pattern established by Jacob Bronowski in his series *The Ascent of Man*, about the history of science and human society, and Kenneth Clark's *Civilization*, a history of Western art, philosophy, and culture. Sagan and Lee changed the series's name to the more secular *Man and the Cosmos*. Finding the new title sexist, Druyan argued they ought to call the series simply *Cosmos*. Druyan also suggested making the series a bit more gender-balanced by focusing on the ancient Greek scientist Hypatia.

Lee and Sagan assembled a team of old friends to work on the scripts, as well as *Ascent of Man* director Adrian Malone. Druyan and Sagan moved out to Los Angles to work on the show, bringing Sagan's trusty secretary and assistant, Shirley Arden, with them.

After an intensive scripting process, Sagan flew around the world to shoot scenes, skipping between India, Greece, England, and the United States. It wasn't always easy. Although Sagan was accustomed to juggling many different responsibilities, he found himself overwhelmed between producing *Cosmos* and keeping up with his writing, editing, and teaching responsibilities—plus his contentious divorce from Linda. To make matters worse, Sagan was a micro-manager who sometimes offended the professionals he worked with by second-guessing them. Tensions ran high on the set.

Still, Sagan's perfectionism allowed him to create a television classic. Sure, some special effects are dated, and the series's pace is a bit slow by today's standards—but much of *Cosmos* is as relevant and exciting as ever.

The series begins with the Big Bang, then takes viewers on a voyage through the known universe to our solar system and our Earth. The origins of life on Earth and evolution are covered, as well as astronomical topics like comets and asteroids, the history of humans' fascination with Mars, and space exploration. *Cosmos* explores atomic structures and the formation of galaxies alike, plus human intelligence, artificial intelligence, and the future of human civilization.

Cosmos premiered in 1980 and became a massive hit, reaching over five hundred million viewers worldwide. From 1980 until 1990, it was public television's most-watched series. It won an Emmy Award and a Peabody Award. The series has been broadcast in over sixty countries worldwide, and it has been updated and rebroadcast several times over the last few decades.

But even this series had its detractors. Some scientists found the series pompous and felt that with this production, Sagan had ceased being a scientist and had become a pure showman. Some religious viewers were upset by the series's blatant atheism.

The book that Sagan wrote to accompany the *Cosmos* series was far better received. The critically acclaimed *Cosmos* book spent seventy weeks on the *New York Times* Best Sellers list. In 1991, *Astronomy* magazine called *Cosmos* "one of the best popular books on astronomy ever written."

CONTACT (1985)

The success of *Cosmos* opened up the doors of Hollywood to Sagan. In 1981, Sagan was given a $2 million advance (the largest ever paid up until that time for a still-unwritten novel) to write a science fiction novel called *Contact*.

Sagan's novel, *Contact*, drew on his scientific interests and personal history to create a story about faith and science. The main character was Dr. Eleanor "Ellie" Arroway, a SETI radioastronomer deeply engaged in the search for extraterrestrial intelligence. A fierce atheist, she clashes with (somewhat simplistically written) religious fundamentalists. One day, Ellie receives an extra-terrestrial message. Decoding it, she discovers directions for building a fantastical machine that transports her and representatives of a few other countries through a "wormhole" in time and space to the very center of the Milky Way. There, aliens appear to each human visitor as a person who means something important to them. Ellie's alien comes to her in the guise of her dead father, who passed away when she was very young. The aliens speak with Ellie about the system of wormholes connecting the universe, telling her that they were created by a long-dead species. But when Ellie returns home, her team discovers that the video evidence they took of their encounter has been erased. They cannot prove that their alien encounter ever occurred. Nobody believes them.

The later movie adaptation of *Contact* (1997) ends the story here, on an unresolved note that forces our scientific heroine to realize that sometimes faith is necessary to make sense of life on this planet. However, that is not where Sagan's novel ends. He has Ellie follow a tip from the aliens to discover that the number pi actually contains a pattern, a secret code. Because pi is one of the most fundamental numbers in creation, this code means a benevolent intelligence has had a deep hand in designing the universe.

Contact sold nearly two million copies and reached an even wider audience when it was made into a major motion picture, directed by Robert Zemeckis and starring Jodie Foster.

Sagan and Druyan worked hard on adapting his book into a screenplay, making a number of changes in order to streamline the plot and make it more dramatic.

The movie *Contact* premiered a few months after Sagan's death. It was not a bomb, but it also wasn't a huge box office hit. This was partially because it was pitted at movie theaters against two huge summer blockbusters, *Men in Black* and *Independence Day*—one a comedy in which aliens secretly exist on Earth but must be hidden from humans and the other a violent movie about alien invasion.

LATER BOOKS

After creating his *Cosmos* series, Sagan went on to write several other important books. Throughout all of them, he slowly shifted his focus from the stars to the earth.

The book *The Cold and the Dark: the World After Nuclear War* (1985) reflected Sagan's deep concern with nuclear power and explored the theory of nuclear winter.

The *Shadows of Forgotten Ancestors: A Search for Who We Are* (1993), cowritten with Ann Druyan, considers how both negative and positive human traits—such as consciousness, territoriality, ethnocentrism, xenophobia, submission to authority, and reason—may have developed as a part of our species's evolution. Although *Shadows of Forgotten Ancestors* was not a huge hit like Sagan's earlier works, today many consider this to be one of his best books.

The Demon-Haunted World: Science as a Candle in the Dark (1996) is a celebration of the scientific method, critical thinking skills, and skepticism in general. Sagan introduces his "baloney detection kit" method of thinking skeptically about wild ideas. Sagan also discusses all of his own speculations, ideas, and theories that have been disproven by science.

Billions and Billions: Thoughts on Life and Death at the Brink of the Millennium (1997) was Sagan's last book; in fact, he did not live to see it published. It collected essays about a wide range of timely topics including the population explosion, politics, and global warming. Sagan also discusses the disease, myelodysplasia, that would kill him. It was personal yet grandiose, epic yet intimate, soaring and practical—a perfect prose encapsulation of the different impulses that Sagan juggled his entire life and brought together in order to enlighten the world.

CHAPTER SIX

SAGAN THE ADVOCATE

A s his career progressed, his fame grew, and his health deteriorated, Sagan grew more and more interested in spreading a few important messages. He spoke out against pseudoscientists, hoaxers, and hucksters whose claims sounded scientific but crumbled under closer examination. And he warned the world about the dangers of nuclear war, which he feared might render our home planet, the "pale blue dot," uninhabitable.

SCIENTIFIC METHOD

Throughout his career, Sagan made a point of debating and debunking pseudoscientists. For instance, he spoke out against the nonsense ideas of Immanuel Velikovsky, who claimed that Venus had originally been a comet that shot out from the planet Jupiter,

Sagan giving a talk about *Voyager 2* at NASA's Jet Propulsion Laboratories in 1986. Sagan loved to give talks to the public and was in high demand as a speaker throughout his career.

passed Earth, causing ancient cataclysms recorded in our holy scriptures, before settling into its orbit today and becoming a planet. In the gullible atmosphere of the late sixties and early seventies, Velikovsky managed to garner a large number of supporters. Against the advice of some of his stuffier colleagues, Sagan actually publicly debated Velikovsky, using the opportunity to educate his audience about the scientific method.

THE BALONEY DETECTION KIT

Sagan was fond of saying that extraordinary claims require extraordinary evidence. In his book *The Demon-Haunted World*, Sagan introduced a concept he called his "baloney detection kit," a series of tools that anyone could use to see whether an argument or an idea might be true or whether it might belong to the realm of faith, fallacy, or scam.

A few of the tools from Sagan's baloney detection included:

- Any hypothesis should be able to be tested. It's important that an idea should be *falsifiable*—others should be able to use a test or experiment to show that an idea is false. Don't trust claims that can't be tested or falsified.
- Facts should be independently verified whenever possible. When a scientific experiment is sound, others should be able to duplicate it, repeating the experiment and achieving the same results.
- In science, facts are more important than beliefs. Statements from authority figures or experts do not count as facts.
- To answer a question, many different hypotheses should be considered and tested. Don't favor your own hypotheses over those of others.

- Use Occam's razor: when you have two different hypotheses capable of explaining the same set of data, favor the simpler explanation.

The baloney detection kit also included a set of guidelines for using reason, logic, and rhetoric to make sound arguments. These included avoiding ad hominem attacks that dismiss an argument by discrediting the person making the argument and using small samples to support your argument ("statistics of small numbers").

ANTINUCLEAR ACTIVIST

Perhaps Sagan's most passionate campaign was his work against nuclear weapons. In order to understand the bravery and urgency of Sagan's stance, it's important to know something about the context of the early 1980s.

THE COLD WAR REIGNITES

With the election of Ronald Reagan in 1980, America swung to the right on a variety of issues. Social and religious conservatives held the day in Congress, while the administration was full of defense "hawks" who favored a more aggressive stance toward the U.S.S.R. Reagan talked tough, calling the U.S.S.R. an "evil empire" and predicting that it would soon be consigned to the "ash-heap of history." He also initiated a huge buildup of the United States military, intensifying the arms race with the U.S.S.R. Nuclear war between the superpowers suddenly seemed a lot more likely.

Sagan was a staunch opponent of nuclear weapons in general. Once he drafted an important petition opposing President Reagan's Strategic Defense Initiative (the nuclear program popularly known as "Star Wars") even though he was seriously ill in the hospital. But Sagan truly put the full force of his fame behind spreading the word about the theory of nuclear war.

NUCLEAR WINTER

In the 1980s, many U.S. strategists believed that it was theoretically possible to "win" a nuclear war. While any exchange of nuclear weapons between the U.S. and U.S.S.R. would lead to absolutely horrific casualties on both sides, at the end one victor would be left standing. This pronuclear assumption was challenged by the idea of nuclear winter.

The theory of nuclear winter was formed by a small group of scientists: Richard Turco, Brian Toon, Thomas Ackerman, and Jim Pollack. Together with Sagan, the group referred to itself as TTAPS. It all began when Toon presented a scientific paper at a 1981

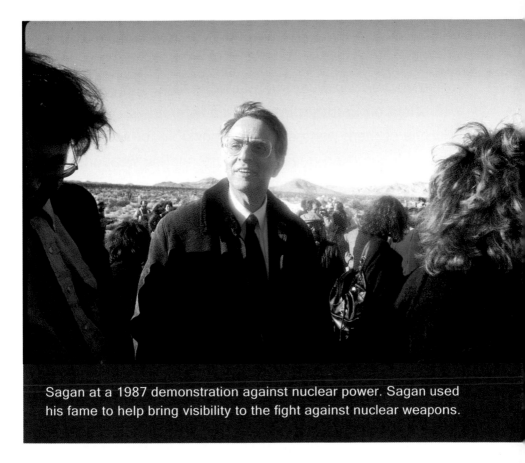

Sagan at a 1987 demonstration against nuclear power. Sagan used his fame to help bring visibility to the fight against nuclear weapons.

conference entitled "Geological Implications of Large Asteroids and Comets on the Earth." He touched on the idea—little known at the time—that the dinosaurs had been wiped out after a huge asteroid hit the earth, kicking up enough dust to change the planet's climate for a short but significant period of time, causing mass extinctions. After his talk, Toon was approached by the National Academy of Sciences (NAS). They asked Toon to study whether a similarly catastrophic effect could be triggered by a nuclear war.

80

Toon and his collaborator Turco were reluctant to take on the assignment at first. They assumed that a nuclear war would not have the same devastating effect on Earth's climate as an asteroid—and neither one of them wanted to be responsible for writing a study that said it was OK to use nuclear weapons. But as they investigated the question proposed by the NAS, they were surprised and terrified by what they found.

TTAPS eventually worked out a model for a scenario that they called nuclear winter. In a nuclear war in which several major cities are destroyed (claiming millions of casualties worldwide), the black soot from burning cities, full of blazing plastics and petroleum products, darkens the skies and blacks out the sun. Beneath this dark radioactive cloud, temperatures plunge. Winds blow the cloud across Earth. With every day that the sun doesn't reach Earth's surface, Earth gets colder and colder. Frost and lack of sunlight destroy crops. Livestock die. Survivors starve. The "winner" of the nuclear war emerges to rule over a hellish landscape of blight, famine, and death.

This nuclear winter scenario was so dramatic that at first it seemed unbelievable. But as they reviewed their data, TTAPS found that their numbers weren't going away. Even a limited nuclear war could have absolutely catastrophic consequences for the entire globe.

In this 1985 photo, Sagan testifies about nuclear winter before the U.S. Congress's House Science and Technology Subcommittee on Natural Resources.

The NASA-Ames Research Center sponsors of TTAPS's research knew that the Reagan administration wouldn't be happy with these findings and they feared having their funding slashed. The agency tried to bury the group's findings, denying them the peer review that would give their research legitimacy. So Sagan sidestepped NASA, organizing an alternate peer review process by calling together a number of experts on the climate and nuclear weapons to meet and discuss the research. According to an article by

CONTROVERSIAL SAGAN

Almost from the very beginning of his career, Sagan was resented by some scientists who didn't like how cozy he was with the media. Some questioned his scientific rigor, or the significance of his scientific achievements. Others felt that Sagan was arrogant and self-satisfied. Sagan sometimes played into this perception—for instance, his curriculum vitae (or scientific résumé) was over one full inch (2.5 centimeters) thick and listed every single talk Sagan had ever given, no matter how tiny the audience, and every article in every single newspaper that discussed his work. And of course, more than a few scientists were jealous of Sagan's success, his money, and his fame.

Thanks to these negative feelings, Sagan was snubbed by the most important scientific organization in the United States, the National Academy of Sciences.

Anybody who was anybody in the world of American science belonged to NAS: being invited to join was a very big deal. However, when Sagan was put up for membership, his candidacy was voted down. Sagan's first wife, Lynn Margulis, was a member, and she participated in the debate over Sagan's candidacy. According to *Carl Sagan: A Life* by biographer Keay Davidson, Lynn reported back to Sagan: "They are jealous of your communication skills, charm, good looks and outspoken attitude, especially on nuclear winter... in summary, you deserved election to the National Academy years ago and still do; it is the worst of human frailties that keeps you out: jealousy."

In 1994, the National Academy of Sciences compensated in part for this snub by awarding Sagan the prestigious Public Welfare Medal, in recognition of all that Sagan had done to popularize science.

Bruce Fellman in the *Scientist* magazine, he told the gathering, "I deeply wish that what I am about to tell you were only a ghost story, something invented to frighten children for a day. But unfortunately, it is not just a story."

The nuclear winter idea spread quickly and was taken up by many antinuclear activists. However, it had its opponents. Of course there were the nuclear hawks, who sponsored rival research to poke holes in the theory. Then there were peace activists who worried that the idea of nuclear winter sent the world the wrong message about the morality of nuclear war.

After all, if millions of people were killed worldwide by nuclear war, wasn't that reason enough to oppose nuclear weapons? If the debate became all about the potential winter caused by a nuclear war, what was to prevent the military from simply developing nuclear weapons like neutron bombs that could kill millions, but leave buildings intact?

Sagan remained steadfast in his mission to spread the idea of nuclear winter and to oppose nuclear weapons in general. 1n 1986, Sagan even went to the Nevada nuclear test site to protest and was arrested along with over a hundred other protesters.

Opposition to nuclear war made strange bed-fellows. Pope John Paul II invited Sagan, a noted atheist, to the Vatican for a briefing on nuclear winter. After their conversation, the Pope made a statement condemning nuclear war and warning of the possibility of nuclear winter.

SAGAN'S LEGACY

A t times, Sagan seemed tireless, writing, teaching, appearing on television, flying around the country and the world. The workload would have been difficult for many healthy people. It's even more impressive when you learn that for much of his later life, Sagan was actually very ill.

STRUGGLES WITH ILLNESS

From the age of eighteen on, Sagan suffered from achalasia. This disorder causes the esophagus to clench, causing problems with swallowing and sometimes even breathing. It's a rare disease, affecting only one person out of every one hundred thousand. The condition plagued Sagan throughout his life and shaped much of his behavior. Sagan would cut his food into very small pieces, and sometimes he would jump up and down after meals, trying to coax food

down his throat. The condition might have been partially caused or exacerbated by the extreme amount
of pressure Sagan put on himself.

Sagan attempted various remedies for his condition. In 1969, he underwent esophageal surgery,
hoping that it might cure his condition. But the
attempt backfired when his lungs filled with blood
after the surgery. Sagan almost died.

FINAL ILLNESS

One day in late 1994, Druyan suddenly noticed
a strange, nasty-looking bruise on Sagan's arm. It
turned out that Sagan had a rare blood disorder
named myelodysplasia. His bone marrow wasn't making enough normal blood cells to supply his body.
The condition would have to be treated with a bone
marrow transplant. Luckily Sagan's sister, Cari, was a
willing bone marrow donor.

Sagan underwent painful treatments at Seattle's
Fred Hutchinson Cancer Research Center. Even after
the disease seemed under control, Druyan and Sagan
regularly flew back and forth from Ithaca, where
Sagan still taught at Cornell, to Seattle.

Sagan kept writing and producing. Illness turned
him inward a bit and made him more focused on
family. He was a man with a mission, but also a man
who had glimpsed his own mortality.

But the treatments were hard on Sagan. In just a few years, Sagan was bone-thin, wasting away from the chemotherapy treatments involved in the transplant process. According to Sagan's biographer Keay Davidson, in *Carl Sagan: A Life*, toward the end of his life Sagan was interviewed by journalist Ted Koppel. A little shocked to see how ill Sagan looked, Koppel asked him whether illness had given him any insights. Sagan thought, and then replied: "These are our true circumstances. We live on a tiny ball of rock and dust, in a cosmos vast beyond our imagining."

In late 1996, Sagan fell ill and had to be rushed back to Seattle. There, his doctors discovered that Sagan had somehow contracted pneumonia. His body was hardly strong enough to fight off the illness; it was obvious that Sagan was not long for this world. Sagan's friends and family traveled to his side or called to say goodbye. Druyan was with her husband until the very end. As she later described his death in her epilogue to Sagan's last book, *Billions and Billions*: "Brave man, wonderful man," I said to him over and over. "Well done. With pride and joy in our love, I let you go. Without fear. June 1. June 1. For keeps…"

On December 20, 1996, Carl Sagan finally succumbed to his illness. He was just sixty-two years old.

PALE BLUE DOT SPEECH

In our introduction, we mentioned the famous "pale blue dot" photograph taken by the *Voyager* space probe from the outer limits of the universe. Here are Sagan's thoughts on seeing Earth from billions of miles away, as delivered in a 1994 lecture at Cornell and as transcribed in his book, *Pale Blue Dot: A Vision of the Human Future in Space*:

> On it, everyone you ever heard of...The aggregate of all our joys and sufferings, thousands of confident religions, ideologies and economic doctrines, every hunter and forager, every hero and coward, every creator and destroyer of civilizations, every king and peasant, every young couple in love, every hopeful child, every mother and father, every inventor and explorer, every teacher of morals, every corrupt politician, every superstar, every supreme leader, every saint and sinner in the history of our species, lived there on a mote of dust, suspended in a sunbeam.
> [...]
> Think of the rivers of blood spilled by all those generals and emperors so that in glory and triumph they could become the momentary masters of a fraction of a dot.
> [...]

The famous Pale Blue Dot photo, taken four billion miles away from Earth. This is just one detail of the picture, magnified so that you can see Earth, the pale blue dot in the yellow band of light. The larger image shows Saturn and its rings.

To me, it underscores our responsibility to deal more kindly with one another and to preserve and cherish the pale blue dot, the only home we've ever known.

A STAR DISAPPEARS

Sagan's death at such a young age caught many by surprise. He had been one of the world's foremost advocates for science. It seemed cruel that he had been taken at such a young age, when he still had so much to contribute to the world.

The *New York Times* ran Sagan's lengthy obituary on its front page, an honor reserved for very few notable individuals. Sagan was honored at three packed memorials: one in Ithaca, one in Pasadena, and one in New York City's Saint John the Divine Cathedral. Speakers at the New York City funeral included Sagan's son Jeremy, who spoke thoughtfully about his father's passions, his advocacy, and his commitment to social justice, and Vice President Al Gore.

Posthumous tributes rolled in. The American Astronomical Society's Division of Planetary Sciences, which Sagan helped to found, posthumously awarded him its highest honor, the Kuiper Prize. Sagan's adopted home town, the city of Ithaca, New York, created the Carl Sagan Memorial Planet Walk. In the city's downtown area, visitors can wander through a scale model of the universe, where sculptures represent the planets, their distances from each other teaching casual passersby about their location in the universe.

The Carl Sagan Memorial Planet Walk is the town of Ithaca, New York's tribute to Sagan. Sagan lived and worked in Ithaca while teaching at Cornell.

Since Sagan's death, Druyan has continued writing and carried on her late husband's work. For instance, she collected *Varieties of Scientific Experience: A Personal View of the Search for God* (2006), sharing some of Sagan's unpublished lectures. In 2009, Druyan launched a series of video podcasts filmed at her home called *At Home in the Cosmos with Annie Druyan*. In the mid-2010s, Druyan was also working with *Cosmos* coproducer Steven Soter to create a *Cosmos* reboot, starring famous astronomer Neil deGrasse Tyson.

Neil deGrasse Tyson and Ann Druyan discuss their upcoming production, *Cosmos: A Spacetime Odyssey*, in October 2013. Tyson has followed in Sagan's footsteps as one of astronomy's great popularizers.

NASA also found a way to honor Sagan. The formal name of the spacecraft lander that delivered the 1997 *Sojourner* robotic rover to the surface of Mars is the Carl Sagan Memorial Station.

Perhaps most beautifully, both Sagan and Druyan have small asteroids named after them. As long as humans study outer space, they will be remembered.

Sagan lived his life passionately. He researched, speculated, and dreamed. He fought fiercely for what he believed in, crusading fearlessly against pseudoscience and taking courageous stands against Jim Crow, the Vietnam War, and, above all, against nuclear war. But perhaps more important, Sagan inspired generations of ordinary Americans to care more deeply about science, about the universe, and about Earth. Perhaps you will become one of those young people whose lives are touched by his work.

TIMELINE

November 9, 1934 Carl Sagan is born to Rachel and Sam Sagan.

1939 Young Carl Sagan attends, and is inspired by, the New York World's Fair.

1941 Carl's sister, Carol "Cari" Mae Sagan, is born.

1948 The Sagan family moves from Brooklyn to Rahway, New Jersey.

1952 Sagan works with geneticist H. J. Muller.

1954 Sagan earns his A.B. with honors from the University of Chicago.

1955 Sagan earns his B.S. in physics from the University of Chicago.

1956 Sagan earns his master of science degree and works with astronomer Gerard Kuiper at McDonald Observatory in Fort Davis, Texas.

1957 Sagan works with physicist George Gamow at the University of Colorado.

June 16, 1957 Sagan marries Lynn Alexander (now known as Lynn Margulis).

October 4, 1957 The Soviet Union launches *Sputnik*, the first man-made satellite.

1959 Sagan's first son, Dorion Solomon Sagan, is born.

1960 Sagan earns his Ph.D. in astronomy and astrophysics from the University of Chicago and moves to Berkeley to take the prestigious Miller Fellowship. Sagan's second son, Jeremy Ethan Sagan, is born.

1962 Lynn Sagan leaves her husband, ending Sagan's first marriage. *Mariner 2* probe studies the atmosphere of Venus. Sagan becomes an assistant professor of astronomy at Harvard.

1963 Sagan travels to Alabama to protest Jim Crow segregation laws.

1966 Sagan resigns from the U.S. Air Force Scientific Advisory Board's Geophysics Panel, citing his opposition to the Vietnam War. Sagan publishes *The Planets* and *Intelligent Life in the Universe*.

1968 Sagan marries Linda Salzman. Sagan joins the astronomy faculty at Cornell University.

1969 The United States puts a man on the moon during the *Apollo 11* moon landing.

1970 Sagan's son Nicholas Julian Zapata Sagan is born. The *Pioneer 10* and *Pioneer 11* spacecraft carry plaques bearing a special message partially devised by Sagan and his wife Linda into space.

1971 Sagan is awarded tenure at Cornell University.

1973 Sagan's book *The Cosmic Connection* is published, and he makes his first appearance on Johnny Carson's *Tonight Show*.

1974 Sagan and his future wife, Ann Druyan, meet at a dinner party thrown by film director Nora Ephron. Sagan helps to write the Arecibo message, beamed into space from the Arecibo Observatory in Puerto Rico.

1977 Sagan leaves his wife Linda for Ann Druyan. The *Voyager* Golden Record is sent into space. Sagan's book *The Dragons of Eden* wins the Pulitzer Prize.

1979 Sagan publishes *Broca's Brain: Reflections on the Romance of Science*.

1980 Sagan's groundbreaking television series *Cosmos* premieres. Sagan cofounds the Planetary Society. Ronald Reagan is elected president of the United States.

1981 Sagan's divorce from Linda is finalized. Druyan and Sagan are married on June 1.

1982 Sagan's daughter, Alexandra "Sasha" Druyan, is born.

1985 Sagan's novel, *Contact*, is published.

1986 Sagan protests at Nevada Nuclear Test Site.

1990 The famous "pale blue dot" photo of Earth as it appears from the limits of our Solar System is taken.

1991 Sagan's youngest son, Samuel Democritus Sagan, is born.

1993 Sagan's book *The Shadows of Forgotten Ancestors: A Search for Who We Are*, is published.

1994 Sagan publishes *Pale Blue Dot: A Vision of the Human Future in Space*. Sagan is diagnosed with myelodysplasia. He also wins the National Academy of Science's Public Welfare Medal.

1996 Sagan publishes *The Demon-Haunted World: Science as a Candle in the Dark*.

December 20, 1996 Carl Sagan dies.

1997 Sagan's book *Billions and Billions: Thoughts on Life and Death at the Brink of the Millenium* is published. The movie *Contact* premieres. The robotic *Sojourner* rover lands on Mars in the Carl Sagan Memorial Station.

GLOSSARY

amino acids Also known as "the building blocks of life," these compounds form the basic components of proteins and are found in plants and animals.

astrophysics A branch of science that applies the laws of physics to the study of the stars.

biosignature An organic substance that provides evidence of life, whether past or present. For instance, the presence of ice on Mars indicates that there may have once been enough water on the red planet to sustain life.

extraterrestrial Anything that exists outside of Earth and its atmosphere.

fellowship An award given by a university, in the form of financial aid, to allow someone to pursue a course of study.

geneticist A scientist who studies genetics, a branch of biological sciences that deals with genes and their heredity from one generation of organisms to the next.

greenhouse effect A term used to describe the process of excess heat becoming trapped within Earth's atmosphere as a result of the increased presence of carbon dioxide, as well as other gases, in the atmosphere.

microorganism An organism that is so tiny its presence can only be detected with the use of a microscope.

National Academy of Sciences A nonprofit organization, established by Abraham Lincoln, that works to advise the United States on various scientific matters.

nuclear winter A hypothetical situation where, following a nuclear war, dust and ash floating in Earth's atmosphere blocks the sun's rays, causing the planet to plunge into a nightmarish winter.

organic molecule Any molecule that contains a significant amount of carbon.

Pale of Settlement In the eighteenth and nineteenth centuries, an area of Imperial Russia where Jews were allowed to live.

pi The ratio of a circle's circumference to its diameter.

pseudoscience A theory or claim that is not supported by sound scientific research.

pulsar A neutron star that emits electromagnetic radiation. The radiation is emitted in a beam, and because the pulsar rotates, it can be detected only intermittently from Earth.

radioastronomy The study of celestial bodies through the use of radio waves.

satire The use of humor and mockery to reveal the shortcomings of individuals or society.

SDI An acronym for Strategic Defense Initiative, a Reagan-era proposal to create an antinuclear missile system that would protect the United States from atomic attacks.

SETI An acronym for the search for extraterrestrial intelligence, which describes a number of projects and activities undertaken by scientists to determine whether or not intelligent life exists in the universe outside of Earth.

terraform A hypothetical process by which an uninhabitable celestial body could be made habitable by human beings.

UFO An acryonym for unidentified flying object; UFOs were frequently reported in the years following World War II and many believed them to be alien spacecraft.

World's Fair A massive, international exposition hosted by a different country every year. The first World's Fair was held in 1850.

FOR MORE INFORMATION

Canadian Space Agency
John H. Chapman Space Centre
6767 Route de l'Aéroport
Saint-Hubert, QC J3Y 8Y9
Canada
(450) 926-4800
Web site: http://www.asc-csa.gc.ca
The Canadian Space Agency is committed to advancing the study and understanding of space through continued research and encourages public interest in space science.

Carl Sagan Center
SETI Institute
189 Bernardo Avenue, Suite 100
Mountain View, CA 94043
(650) 961-6633
Web site: http://www.seti.org/carlsagancenter
The Carl Sagan Center brings together numerous researchers to study all aspects of the possibility of life in the universe, including its beginnings in the universe, the evolution of life-forms, and environments that are hospitable to life—both on Earth and elsewhere in the solar system.

Cornell Astronomy
610 Space Science Building
Ithaca, NY 14853
(607) 255-6920
Web site: http://www.astro.cornell.edu
The Cornell Astronomy Department, of which Carl
    Sagan was a part for many years as a professor, is
    responsible for Cornell University's academic
    program in astronomy. Sagan was also director of
    Cornell's Laboratory for Planetary Studies during
    his tenure.

NASA
Public Communications Office
NASA Headquarters
Suite 2R40
Washington, DC 20546-000
(202) 358-0001
Web site: http://www.nasa.gov
The National Aeronautics and Space Administration
    is a government agency responsible for the United
    States' space program, as well as all other
    branches of its aeronautical research.

National Academy of Sciences
500 Fifth Street NW
Washington, DC 20001

(202) 334-2000

Web site: http://www.nasonline.org

The National Academy of Sciences is a nonprofit
  organization that works to provide advice to the
  United States on scientific matters. Its members
  consist of the world's most distinguished scientists, engineers, and health professionals.

RAND Corporation

1776 Main Street

P.O. Box 2138

Santa Monica, CA 90407-2138

Web site: http://www.rand.org

The RAND Corporation was founded in 1948 to be a
  think tank to advise the U.S. armed forces about
  policy matters. Over the years, the RAND
  Corporation has expanded its scope and now
  works with a variety of other organizations, with a
  continued focus on providing high-quality
  research on a range of social policy issues.

Royal Astronomical Society of Canada

203-4920 Dundas Street W

Toronto, ON M9A IB7

Canada

(416) 924-7973

Web site: http://www.rasc.ca

Originally founded in 1868 as the Toronto
Astronomical Club, the Royal Astronomical Society
of Canada began as a way to encourage public
interest in, and engagement with, astronomy. Today
the society has approximately four thousand
members.

University of Chicago Department of Astronomy and
Astrophysics
5640 S. Ellis Avenue
Chicago, IL 60637
(773) 702-8203
Web site: http://astro.uchicago.edu
The University of Chicago Department of Astronomy
and Astrophysics, from which Carl Sagan obtained
his Ph.D., is responsible for the University of
Chicago's academic program as well as several
international projects in the field of space science.

WEB SITES

Due to the changing nature of Internet links, Rosen
Publishing has developed an online list of Web sites
related to the subject of this book. This site is updated
regularly. Please use this link to access the list:

http://www.rosenlinks.com/GSW/Sagan

FOR FURTHER READING

Aguilar, David A. *13 Planets: The Latest View of the Solar System*. Des Moines, IA: National Geographic Children's Books, 2011.

Angelo, Joseph. *Encyclopedia of Space and Astronomy*. New York, NY: Facts On File, 2006.

Armstrong, Mabel. *Women Astronomers: Reaching for the Stars*. Marcola, OR: Stone Pine Press, 2008.

Bell, Jim. *The Space Book: From the Beginning to the End of Time, 250 Milestones in the History of Space & Astronomy*. New York, NY: Sterling Milestones, 2013.

Couper, Heather, and Nigel Henbest. *Encyclopedia of Space*. New York, NY: DK Children, 2009.

Dinwiddle, Robert, David Hughes, Giles Sparrow, and Carole Stott. *Space: From Earth to the Edge of the Universe*. New York, NY: DK Publishing, 2010.

Dyson, Marianne. *Twentieth Century Space and Astronomy: A History of Notable Research and Discovery*. New York, NY: Facts On File, 2007.

Nardo, Don. *Destined for Space: Our Story of Exploration*. North Mankato, MN: Capstone Press, 2012.

Pogue, William. *How Do You Go to the Bathroom in Space?* New York, NY: Tor Books, 2011.

Pyle, Rod. *Destination Mars: New Explorations of the Red Planet*. Amherst, NY: Prometheus Books, 2012.

Rey, H. A. *The Stars*. New York, NY: HMH Books for Young Readers, 2008.

Sagan, Carl. *Contact*. New York, NY: Pocket Books, 1997.

Sagan, Carl. *Cosmos*. New York, NY: The Ballantine Publishing Group, 2013.

Sagan, Carl. *The Demon-Haunted World: Science as a Candle in the Dark*. New York, NY: Ballantine Books, 1997.

Sagan, Carl. *The Dragons of Eden: Speculations on the Evolution of Human Intelligence*. New York, NY: Ballantine Books, 1986.

Sobel, Dava. *The Planets*. New York, NY: Penguin Books, 2006.

Todd, Deborah, and Joseph Angelo Jr. *A to Z of Scientists in Space and Astronomy*. New York, NY: Facts On File, 2005.

Trefil, James. *Space Atlas: Mapping the Universe and Beyond*. Des Moines, IA: National Geographic, 2012.

Tyson, Neil deGrasse. *Death by Black Hole: And Other Cosmic Quandaries*. New York, NY: W. W. Norton & Company, 2007.

Tyson, Neil deGrasse. *Space Chronicles: Facing the Ultimate Frontier*. New York, NY: W. W. Norton & Company, 2013.

Wildside Press. *The Science Fiction Megapack: 25 Science Fiction Stories by Masters*. Rockville, MD: Wildside Press, 2011.

BIBLIOGRAPHY

Abumrad, Jad, and Robert Krulwich. "Carl Sagan and Ann Druyan's Ultimate Mix Tape." *Radiolab*. WNYC, February 12, 2010. Retrieved September 1, 2013 (http://www.npr.org/2010/02/12/123534818/carl-sagan-and-ann-druyans-ultimate-mix-tape).

Broad, William J. "Even in Death, Carl Sagan's Influence Is Still Cosmic." *New York Times*, December 1, 1998, p. D-5.

Collins, Glenn. "The Sagans: Fiction and Fact Back to Back." *New York Times*, September 30, 1985, p. B-11.

Davidson, Keay. *Carl Sagan: A Life*. New York, NY: John Wiley, 1999.

Drake, Frank, Ann Druyan, Timothy Ferris, and Carl Sagan. *Murmurs of Earth: The Voyager Interstellar Record*. New York, NY: Random House, 1978.

Drake, Frank, and Dava Sobel. *Is Anyone Out There? The Search for Extraterrestrial Intelligence*. New York, NY: Delacorte Press, 1992.

Druyan, Ann, and Carl Sagan. *Shadows of Forgotten Ancestors*. New York, NY: Ballantine Books, 1993.

Ehrlich, Paul R., Carl Sagan, Donald Kennedy, and Walter Orr Roberts, eds. *The Cold and the Dark: The World After Nuclear War*. New York, NY: Norton, 1984.

English, Marianna. "How Carl Sagan Worked." HowStuffWorks.com. Retrieved September 1, 2013 (http://science.howstuffworks.com/dictionary/famous-scientists/physicists/carl-sagan.htm).

Fellman, Bruce. "'Nuclear Winter' Comes in from the Cold." *Scientist*, May 1, 1989. Retrieved September 1, 2013 (http://www.the-scientist.com/?articles.view/articleNo/10342/title/-Nuclear-Winter--Comes-In-From-The-Cold).

Golden, Frederic. "Showman of Science." *Time*, October 20, 1980, pp. 2, 62–69.

Lewontin, Richard. "Review of *The Demon-Haunted World* by Carl Sagan." *New York Review of Books*, January 9, 1997, p. 28.

Menzel, Donald H., and Lyle G. Boyd. *The World of Flying Saucers: A Scientific Examination of a Major Myth of the Space Age.* New York, NY: Doubleday, 1963.

National Geographic. "Mariner Scans a Lifeless Venus." May 1963, p. 733.

New York Times. "Carl Sagan Dies." December 21, 1996, p. 1, 26.

Poundstone, William. *Carl Sagan: A Life in the Cosmos.* New York, NY: Henry Holt and Company, 1999.

Restak, Richard. "The Brain Knew More Than the Genes." *New York Times Book Review*, May 29, 1977, p. 8.

Sagan, Carl. *Billions and Billions: Thoughts on Life and Death at the Brink of the Millennium.* New York, NY: Ballantine Books, 1998.

Sagan, Carl. *Contact.* New York, NY: Pocket Books, 1997.

Sagan, Carl. *The Cosmic Connection: An Extraterrestrial Perspective.* New York, NY: Cambridge University Press, 2000.

Sagan, Carl. *Cosmos.* New York, NY: Ballantine Books, 2011.

Sagan, Carl. *The Demon-Haunted World: Science as a Candle in the Dark.* New York, NY: Ballantine Books, 1997.

Sagan, Carl. *The Dragons of Eden: Speculations on the Evolution of Human Intelligence.* New York, NY: Ballantine Books, 1986.

Sagan, Carl. *Pale Blue Dot: A Vision of the Human Future in Space.* New York, NY: Ballantine Books, 1997.

Sagan, Carl. "The Planet Venus." *Science*, March 24, 1961, p. 849.

Snyder, Dave. "An Observational History of Mars." January 2002. Retrieved September 1, 2013 (http://www.umich.edu/~lowbrows/reflections/2001/dsnyder.7.html).

Spangenburg, Ray. *Carl Sagan: A Biography.* Westport, CT: Greenwood Publishing Group, 2004.

Tyson, Neil deGrasse, and Steven Soter, eds. *Cosmic Horizons: Astronomy at the Cutting Edge.* New York, NY: New Press, 2001.

Wachhorst, Wyn. "Carl Sagan: Visionary." April 18, 2013. Retrieved September 1, 2013 (http://wynwachhorst.com/carl-sagan-visionary).

INDEX

A

achalasia, 85
Ackerman, Thomas, 78
Alexander, Lynn, 25
Apollo, 42–43
Arecibo message, 54–55
Asimov, Isaac, 35

B

Billions and Billions, 73, 87

C

California, University of,
    Berkeley, 30
Calvin, Melvin, 23
Carl Sagan Memorial
    Station, 93
Carson, Johnny, 62–63, 64
Chicago, University of, 17,
    19, 21, 23, 25
Cold and the Dark, The, 72
Cold War, 27, 36, 51, 60,
    77–78
Contact, 70–72
Cornell University, 39–40,
    53, 86, 88
Cosmic Connection, The,
    60–62
Cosmos, 66–70, 72, 92

D

Demon Haunted World, The,
    73, 76

Dragons of Eden, The, 65–66
Drake, Frank, 44, 49, 52, 54
Druyan, Ann, 49, 53,
    55–58, 66, 68, 72, 73,
    86, 87, 92, 93

E

Emmy Award, 69

F

Ferris, Timothy, 49,
    55–56, 58

G

Gamow, George, 23

H

Harvard University, 31–34,
    35, 36, 37–39

I

Icarus, 31
*Intelligent Life in the
    Universe*, 37, 51, 59–60
Interstellar Record, 49–50

K

Khare, Bishun, 31
Kuiper, Gerard, 21
Kuiper Prize, 90

ABOUT THE AUTHOR

Gabrielle Borisovna is an author, playwright, and educator who has been working with young adults for over thirteen years. She has written a number of books on scientific topics, including global warming and science history. She routinely helps students explore scientific topics through essay writing, filmmaking, and research projects.

PHOTO CREDITS